Gobbo:

A Solitaire's Opera

David Cappella

Červená Barva Press
Somerville, Massachusetts

Copyright © 2022 by David Cappella

All rights reserved. No part of this book may be reproduced in any manner without written consent except for the quotation of short passages used inside of an article, criticism, or review.

Červená Barva Press
P.O. Box 440357
W. Somerville, MA 02144-3222

www.cervenabarvapress.com

Bookstore: www.thelostbookshelf.com

Cover art: "One / Leopardi" by Britta Winkels

Cover design: William J. Kelle

ISBN: 978-1-950063-15-4

Library of Congress Control Number: 2022938705

ACKNOWLEDGMENTS

I would like to thank wholeheartedly the following poets, writers, and scholars whose comments helped me see the manuscript through and who had faith that it would see the light of day: Baron Wormser, Jim Provencher, David Daniel, David Durgin, Gray Jacobik, Maria Esposito Frank, Michael Palma, Franco Masciandaro, Leslie McGrath, Steve Ostrowski, and Ravi Shankar. And a very special thanks to my translator Angela D'Ambra whose commitment to the manuscript saw that Giacomo "sang his sorrow" in Italian, Leopardi's native language.

Notes for the following poems in the sequence:

Poems I–X:	Finalist Bordighera Prize, 2006
Poems I–XVII :	Featured, as "The Blue Plate Special" in *Diner*, 2004. Poem I, "Gobbo remembers his youth," nominated for a Pushcart Prize.
Poems I–XXVI:	Bright Hill Press, Poetry Chapbook Contest winner, 2006.
Poems XXV–XXVI:	Scored to music, Composer's Art Songs Symposium, Central Connecticut State University, 2013.
Poem XXVIII:	Appears in *Interno Poesia* as "Infine, Giacomo va via di casa," July 2018, trans. It. Angela D'Ambra.
Poem XXIX:	Appears in *Gradiva 55* as "Giacomo, the traveler" trans. It. Angela D'Ambra.
Poems XXX–XXXIV:	Appear in *Journal of Italian Translation*, Spring 2019, trans. It. Angela D'Ambra
Poems XXXV–XXXIX:	Appear in *Poetarum Silva* trans. It. Angela D'Ambra

Poems LXXX–LXXXIV: featured, *Italian Americana.* Summer, 2014, Vol. XXXII, No. 2.

Poems XCIV–XCVIII: featured in *Ovumque siamo*, Vol. I, Issue 2. Poem XCVIII, "Giacomo, on his corpse," nominated for a Pushcart Prize.

TABLE OF CONTENTS

ACT I

Gobbo remembers his youth…I

Gobbo recollects his childhood, long lost …II

Gobbo muses on his hometown…III

Gobbo muses on his hometown, continued…IV

Gobbo, regarding his years of study…V

Gobbo comments on his love diary…VI

Gobbo describes his first love, the Contessa…VII

Gobbo goes on about his love for the Contessa…VIII

Gobbo realizes he will only imagine love…IX

Gobbo talks about love for Sylvia…X

Gobbo talks about love for Nerina…XI

Gobbo's mother speaks, for the first time …XII

Via letters, Gobbo's first friend…XIII

Finally, after months of delay, Gobbo meets Giordani…XIV

Gobbo's father speaks, for the first time…XV

In his excitement, Gobbo writes two patriotic poems…XVI

Gobbo's two poems receive recognition…XVII

Gobbo himself feels trapped in his home…XVIII

Gobbo fails in his bid for freedom from his father …XIX

Gobbo, silently to his father…XX

Gobbo's father, his soliloquy…XXI

Gobbo's father, his soliloquy continued…XXII

Again, Gobbo despairs…XXIII

Gobbo, the poet…XXIV

Again: Gobbo, the poet...XXV

Gobbo's discontent...XXVI

Gobbo mentions his notebook...XVII

Finally, Gobbo leaves home...XVIII

Gobbo, the traveler...XXIX

On his way to Roma, Gobbo remembers shame...XXX
　　　in Spoleto

Gobbo on his desire and deformity...XXXI

Gobbo contemplates his first trip to Roma...XXXII

In Roma, Gobbo's expectations are shattered...XXXIII

An eminent philologist searches for and finds Gobbo...XXXIV

Gobbo at odds with the world...XXXV

Gobbo makes love to himself...XXXVI

Gobbo weeps at Tasso's grave...XXXVII

Gobbo realizes he will leave Roma...XXXVIII

Homesick, Gobbo bids good-bye to Roma...XXXIX

ACT II

At home, Gobbo turns from poetry to philosophy...XL

An eminent aesthetician discusses Gobbo's philosophy...XLI

Gobbo: *Ex Nihilo*...XLII

Gobbo: *Vox Clamantis in Deserto*...XLIII

Gobbo reflects on his two years at home...XLIV

Gobbo assents to surprise visitors...XLV

Travelling to Milano, Gobbo stops in Bologna...XLVI

Gobbo recounts his winter stay in Bologna...XLVII

Gobbo feels kindness and happiness...XLVIII

A friend comments on the personal habits of Gobbo...XLIX

A friend comment on the unsavory personal habits...L
  of Gobbo

Gobbo reads a poem in public...LI

Gobbo denies being in love with Contessa Teresa...LII

Gobbo reveals his scorn for Contessa Teresa...LIII

Gobbo returns to Palazzo Leopardi...LIV

Gobbo offers sweets instead of stones...LV

Gobbo ventures outside the walls of Palazzo Leopardi...LVI

A friend tells why Gobbo never used sand to dry ink...LVII

In April, Gobbo visits Firenze...LVIII

A literary man offers Gobbo an assignment...LIX

Gobbo refuses the offer of a literary man...LX

Gobbo ponders his seclusion even from friends...LXI

Gobbo articulates his relationship with the world of man...LXII

An enemy attacks Gobbo's work...LXIII

Gobbo endures his suffering and creates more...LXIV

Gobbo describes his meeting with Manzoni...LXV

Gobbo, alone in his room in Firenze...LXVI

Avoiding winter, Gobbo moves to Pisa and finds peace...LXVII

Disappointed, Gobbo's father pleads for his son's return...LXVIII

Gobbo, on his father's love...LXIX

Gobbo, on the attractiveness of Pisa...LXX

While in Pisa, Gobbo muses on the British poets...LXXI

While in Pisa, Gobbo dreams with his eyes open...LXXII

Gobbo writes a poem after years...LXXIII

Now in Firenze, Gobbo sits in a darkened room...LXXIV

Gobbo, on his brother's death and the Holy Sacrament...LXXV

Gobbo meets a man who could have been a real friend...LXXVI
and they discuss poetry

Gobbo recalls his last days in Recanati...LXXVII

Gobbo cut off from his books, from his work...LXXVIII

Gobbo's idleness yields poems...LXXIX

Gobbo leaves home for the last time...LXXX

ACT III

From behind a curtain, Gobbo's father watches his...LXXXI
son leave, never to see him again

Gobbo contemplates being 'Gobbo'...LXXXII

Gobbo flirts with evil...LXXXIII

Gobbo remarks on the last love of his life...LXXXIV

Gobbo recalls clouds and longing...LXXXV

Gobbo, on his friend Ranieri...LXXXVI

Gobbo in Napoli...LXXXVII

Gobbo the neurasthenic...LXXXVIII

Gobbo, alone, experiences the streets of Napoli...LXXXIX

Gobbo, in the writer's café...XC

Gobbo, on some of his weak poems...XCI

A Gobbo scholar recalls one day as a young student...XCII
when Gobbo himself visited the classroom

The same Gobbo scholar recalls his excitement at...XCIII
reading the new edition of Gobbo's poems

Gobbo oscillates between the fear of death and the...XCIV
yearning for it

Gobbo, exhausted and sad...XCV

Gobbo, when his nights were cloudless...XCVI

Ranieri, on Gobbo's last day...XCVII

Gobbo, on his corpse...XCVIII

Nunc Dimittis: Gobbo contemplates his bones...XCIX

In the room where Gobbo was born, his mother...C
     speaks

Note to the Reader

Gobbo: A Solitaire's Opera is a "natural opera." That is, it is the emotional arc of a poet's life rendered in poetry. The sonnet sequence is divided into three acts much like a formal opera, and it is loosely based on the life of the Italian poet, Giacomo Leopardi. His life, fraught with emotional and physical pain, did not stop him from writing some of the most exquisite lyrical poetry of his age, of all time. His view of human nature, of mankind in general was dark, but this was not necessarily because he was physically misshapen, though some think that is the case. Whatever his view of humanity or whatever his emotional and physical pain, Leopardi demonstrated great courage in the face of adversity while his poetry transcended his life.

Though the emotional life of Gobbo follows the life of Leopardi, his voice is, most assuredly, not Leopardi's. The voice of Gobbo is the consciousness of a poet living his life. He is the artist navigating the world. *Gobbo: A Solitaire's Opera* is not an historical or a biographical document.

Gobbo:

A Solitaire's Opera

Act I

I

Gobbo* remembers his youth

Let me tell you about suffering
because I was a boy cold without love
in a large house, so dark it stifled laughs.
I would run to my mother with stones
only to drop them under a grim gaze
so harsh I felt tossed in a freezing bath.
Her words, like a cicada's shrill chirp, pierced
the close air of long summer afternoons.
I remember my brother's folded hands
in the coffin, how I kissed one knuckle.
I cried, torched inside with processional fires
held by shadowed monks cowled in their black walk
through my town's narrow streets,
terrifying my heart forever.

* The Italian word for 'hunchback.'

II

Gobbo recollects his childhood, long lost

As a child, my imagination soared.
I could tie stars to the moon,
hang houses in the sky, stab clouds with my finger.
I was a mad scientist of the dark —
once, late at night, cloistered in the attic,
I lit candles and dangled their long shadows,
conjured phantasmagoric friends.
Fauns slept under haystacks while field girls sang.
Still, my tear stains darkened the bark of trees.
I imagined that Infinity spread
beyond the horizon that fell behind
a distant shepherd's stride. Awestruck, I shuddered.
I could not have friends knowing such terror.
There was no choice but to hide from the world.

III

Gobbo muses on his hometown

My dreams kept me alive. I lived
in that stunted, backward town.
Yes, it had its beauty, sudden little views
where hillsides of olive trees stretched
down to the Adriatic where distant sails
grabbed the breeze and moved slowly away.
And, yes, mountains, layered ranges
of the deepest blue that lifted toward heaven.
So what? I was caged, a captive
of melancholy, ready to jump
head-first into the garden well.
Twenty-one, I had never left town,
never had my own money.
Anguish covered my soul – black scum.

IV

Gobbo muses on his hometown, continued

I hadn't seen anything,
had no experience of the world.
I knew nothing about women.
Body stunting, I lost myself in books
or walked myself silly over the hills
never speaking even to my brother.
The town hated me, and I hated it.
The town's teeth ripped my heart.
The local boys, cursèd wild boars, waited
at the corner to pelt me with snowballs
and yell, "You hermit. You bastard hunchback."
I slunk away. A recluse pays his price.
Still, I recall one cloudless, summer night;
the moon hung serene and golden.

V

Gobbo, regarding his years of study

The library was a monastery;
its books a deathless sanctuary.
As a closeted monk thirsts for heaven,
I drank words, and beside dying candles
I knelt shivering in the cold, my eyes
aching. I came to discover Beauty.
I wrote poems, whispering words to the sky.
I heard the angelic voices of youths
singing "amore." Truly, I was happy.
Yet, during these long years with books I died.
My spine wrinkled up and I couldn't run
with my brother. A girl called me crooked.
Invisible, the cathedral of my inner beauty.
Rage crawled, a rodent in my mind.

VI

Gobbo comments on his love diary

It's true. I did keep a love-diary.
How else could I trap the bear of grief?
I was twenty-one. I was a Romantic.
Women were phantoms traipsing through my dreams.
When I tried to follow, they disappeared
into the ether of immanent sleep
or into patchy fog swirls of waking.
So, I chiseled them, their bodies, in my mind,
sculpted hip curves, full breasts, and pouting lips,
shaping to form what I would never touch.
In my notebook, with the fine cloth of words,
I polished desire as I would a gem.
Love became my private statuary:
marble illusions with forlorn stares.

VII

Gobbo describes his first love, the Contessa

Imagine this: a hunchback, dressed like a priest,
lurking in a shadow, eyes wide
as the Contessa stepped from the carriage.
Her concupiscence devoured my stare;
it ravished every urge. My kiss,
a trembling songbird, alit on her hand.
I dashed away to hide in my room.
She stowed the knowledge of the hump
stuck under my frock behind soothing eyes.
A day later I found words to speak to her.
That evening at dinner, I gazed at her
as though gazing upon a Raphael.
That night, in the drawing room playing chess,
I tried to capture her rooks.

VIII

Gobbo goes on about his love for the Contessa

I won, and she did come to my table,
leaning over me so close that desire
traced a fluttering trail deep within me,
a butterfly trapped inside my bones.
I sat fearful with hope. I froze
in my chair. Suddenly, like moths, others
busily circled the game, dancing
among the soft flames of her eyes.
My pleasure, an invisible smoke,
wafted out of the room and toward the stars.
The next night, when we played alone, I drowned
in anguish even as I made her smile.
Like a riptide, the thought that such pleasure
would vanish hauled me far out from love's shore.

IX

Gobbo realizes he will only imagine love

Sometimes, I think that love is a loom.
Or maybe the sound of a loom
raddled into the voice of a young girl
who sings as she works in the summer heat.
It is never the girl herself, never
anyone particular, only a voice, a smile, a gaze.
Ah Nerina, ah Sylvia,
when I greeted you, the greeting exploded
into shards of piquant fancy, splinters
of desire (yes, I read *Werther*), and I walked
away pursing my lips into a kiss
that I would never give.
Did deliquescent dreams scald me?
No. They were my real love, solid like gold.

X

Gobbo talks about love for Sylvia

I never spied on Sylvia, not once.
Like a May morning she was simply there,
fragrant, fresh, alive. My heart lifted high,
beating furiously, circling, wheeling
above her pristine voice as I sat reading.
When the words in the classics I loved so
bothered me, like crows pestering a hawk,
I gazed out the window, spotted that smile
trapped in the weaving room across the square.
I yearned to swoop down and carry
it up to the lonely aerie of my thoughts
where human sounds faded to echoes.
When I heard she died, my dreams of her paled
into ghostly voices I could not hear.

XI

Gobbo talks about love for Nerina

No one knows who Nerina is, no one.
She was a glimpse in my mind, a glance
as lightning suddenly illuminates
the shape of a tree in dark countryside.
She stands outlined in the thin starlight
of my mind's moonless sky, no longer real.
Did I ever know her? Could I ever?
I truly believe that she greeted my words
outside of town one May evening. Her smile
strolled with me throughout the night, and I dreamt
that I gently kissed her outstretched hand. But
Nerina is dead; her love a sad dream.
I stand before an empty window,
my gaze as lifeless as poor Nerina.

XII

Gobbo's mother speaks, for the first time

God governed my life. It was His glory
that lifted my thoughts into His Kingdom.
My piety stood tall, a stiff sentry,
and guarded the iron gates of my heart.
When one of my children died, I rejoiced,
its cherub-soul floating up to heaven
blossomed like an acacia in my faith.
We are frail; we do have feelings. Mine swam,
those black schools of fish in opaque waters.
How else explain the weeping fits that burst
upon me like a spring shower, sending
me scurrying for shelter in my room?
I suffer still, a burnt tongue, so I pray
God forgives him, that my ugly son dies.

XIII

Via letters, Gobbo's first friend

For hours, I walked and walked the hills alone –
days without books; days alone with my thoughts.
A brush fire flamed within; hazy smoke
of melancholy blurred my solitude.
But a man wrote to me. His letter twined
tendrilled affection around my heart
as an older brother might drape an arm
across my shoulders and squeeze them.
You must remember that I had no one,
no loves, no friends, nothing, just my studies.
I inhaled friendship as one does the air.
I depended upon his advice.
Thus, Giordani became my atmosphere
and with each breath I longed to meet my friend.

XIV

Finally, after months of delay, Gobbo meets Giordani

For the first time ever, I left the house
unescorted and walked backstreets to meet
my friend. When I turned one corner, I froze.
There, almost bumping me, stood my father.
His eyes narrowed, his rebuke punctured
my heart. I trudged home in stinging silence,
as though punctured by the fangs of a snake.
Later, when father's control slithered away
I finally met Giordani. How our talk billowed,
the fair-weather clouds of our thoughts drifting
over the terrain. Our conversation
sailed far past orthodoxy's breakwater.
My friend's stay ended with us alone
on a day trip to Macerata. Joy.

XV

Gobbo's father speaks, for the first time

A storm surge of bitterness rose so fast,
I admit, my resentment rolled in, pounding
upon the bluffs of my love. I hated
this 'friend.' He was a thief; he stole my son.
I am not ashamed, and I feel no guilt.
My son's life is mine: at least it was once.
I regret allowing my son to travel
alone one day with that…that 'apostate.'
Hindsight, a useless balm, only moistens
but does not dampen the pain.
This man's ideas tainted my son's mind
with feckless dreams. They were like germs to me.
I no longer know my son. Who is he?
My throat tightens. I cannot swallow. I…

XVI

In his excitement, Gobbo writes two patriotic poems

Sure, I changed – the age beckoned; I hiked in
its strange forest and followed fresh wolf tracks.
Giordani's talk spurred me deep into woods
so enchanting that I wrote two new poems.
I had spent years toting the luggage of words
owned by others; now I carried my own.
I tried to glorify Italia
galloping forward with her lost banner.
I managed to publish these verses. My canti
fell on their knees, raising their swaddled dreams
skyward in the hope that they would be kissed
by the lips of soldiers, clandestine patriots,
who would fight to make their land one country.
Yes, Poetry conspires with History.

XVII

Gobbo's two poems receive recognition

Did you know that my mischievous songs
traveled over the countryside
like orphans, only to be adopted
by dedicated freedom fighters housed
in the towns of my fragmented homeland?
Did you know, for the first time since Petrarch,
that poems loudly trumpeted "Italia?"
Did you know a decade after I died
young Neapolitans stood at my tomb
with heads bowed, reciting stanzas?
Did you know that Garibaldi's men fanned
the flames of their faith with lines from my poems?
History makes its own pilgrimages;
Poetry can only kiss it good luck.

XVIII

Gobbo feels himself trapped in his home

Cold marble, crouching *prigioniero**
of Michelangelo, movement snared fast,
I did not break free. I trembled apart
from the world. In the cold library, cloaked
in rugs, I gazed from this cell toward the square,
windblown and deserted except for one
dour-faced signora scurrying to church.
Bitterly, I turned back to my studies.
My eyes swelled. I was blinded,
my sight clouded so that words disappeared
into fog as gray as the valley mist
that sweeps up and slowly blots this town.
Blind, caged, almost twenty-one,
I despised Father. I wanted the world.

* Prisoner

XIX

Gobbo fails in his bid for freedom from his father

I had no choice but to try to break free.
Father was my warden, feeding rations
of necessity to me: clothes, food, books,
enough to remain alive, yet he was dead
to my desires as a young man: women
and their company, the men of letters
who knew me, who had opinions of me.
I wanted to celebrate life with work.
I tried to use words to file through
the bars of Father's home and flee, unseen,
to Milano. I procured my passport
through a letter's deceit. My father's friend,
in innocence, delivered it to him.
Thus, my Fate was as twisted as my spine.

XX

Gobbo, silently to his father

Oh, my Father, my Father, my Father.
Everything you've asked of me I have done.
For family, you sacrificed my life:
I drowned myself in books, my spine more warped.
Now mottled by the ringworm of *noia**,
my imagination stabs at my heart
like a pitch-forked daemon jabs at souls
lost in hell. I am nothing but a rat
hugging the shadows of Recanati.
Why, Father, do you expect me to dwell
in this mausoleum of ancestry?
I cannot abide by your wishes now.
I need to walk strange streets, to breathe new air.
I refuse your sly gift of family.

* This Italian word is best described by the French word, *ennui*: the
OED defines ennui as the feeling of mental weariness and
dissatisfaction produced by want of occupation, or by lack of
interest in present surroundings or employments.

XXI

Gobbo's father, his soliloquy

I am no despot. I'm Italian,
head of my household, an aristocrat
in a small town. My sword sways at my side.
This is out of fashion but noble.
Pig-headed, why yes; indecisive, true.
But I love books; I made a library
unrivalled in the land. I am no fool.
I do keep money hidden from my wife.
Once I took off my pants
and gave them to a beggar. The clergy,
at times, is not protected from my wrath.
Who can trust the ideas one hears now?
Blasphemy is the preferred local wine.
My son drank all that was offered him.

XXII

Gobbo's father, his soliloquy continued

How can I understand him? In what way?
He truly hates me; our sundered natures
stand opposed like two peaks, distant and steep,
cloud-covered, rising above the vast gulf
sprawled between them – wide, silent and cold.
I need my son's love, but I will not beg
for it. He must have known that every word
in my letters searched for morsels of trust.
And though none dropped on my plate, I loved him,
my eccentric miracle. His genius,
so precious, so mysterious to me,
stung often, though never poisoned. Like those
foreign languages he spoke and read,
his genius was exotic. I was not.

XXIII

Again, Gobbo despairs

Father pilloried me in daily life.
I could not escape. My hopes soon flitted
away from me like a flock of starlings
darting from dark thickets as dusk descends.
My rheumy eyes, glaucoused with fear, saw white.
I remained a shackled solitary.
My listless body, a boulder, numbed me.
My vision of myself: complete madman
sitting in my study, wide bulging eyes
staring into space, mouth agape, barely
breathing, unable to laugh or to cry,
sunk into the chair of Nothingness, sick
with life. My imagination shriveled.
I kissed my grief, wishing it had real lips.

XXIV

Gobbo, the poet

All of this and, still inside of me, dawn
broke. Its light fanned upward through my heart's clouds.
They floated like roseate words, drifting
across the landscape of my thinking.
The years of hoarding study and reading
left me a scholarly miser, fervent
to caress each word that I discovered.
Language became my exchequer, its coins
prized words that I gleefully stacked, counted
several times over and over. Words —
acqua minerale, clear spring water.
Thirsting, I swallowed them in huge gulps
that livened my blood and freshened my heart.
My sanctity glistened — moistened by words.

XXV

Again: Gobbo, the poet

My despair never lay fallow.
Onto its dark soil, I broadcast vignettes.
These grew into lonely hills, moonlit nights,
sacred moments in fields after rain ends.
I captured in my journal, staccato,
life in my town, a life I could relish
only from the window of my study
where I stood, gazing down at a world closed
forever to me. My loneliness waxed
like the thin moon low in the cloudless sky.
Imagine: the first firefly of summer
languidly floating, the mind exhaling
its thin breath into the thick evening.
My poetry lingers, a silence.

XXVI

Gobbo's discontent

Father choked on my poems. He spat them out.
I choked, too. I coughed up my dreams. I left
myself empty-stomached, starved to leave home.
My work: no balsam for his palette.
He tried to stop every chance to print them.
I was forced to eat this interference
every day. It tasted of dried weeds.
At his dinner table, I fidgeted
with my paper knife and I kept quiet.
The meals set before me nourished nothing.
I was served plates heaped with misery;
I swallowed large bites of indignity,
ceaselessly chewing it into a mush,
pulpy gruel which I gulped silently.

XXVII

Gobbo mentions his notebook

I spent all my time writing to myself.
Pages and pages and then more pages
spilled out of me. A mélange of passion,
grief, despair, insight, poetry –
my solitary life, myself alone –
a commentary on constricted life.
My head pounded, my nerves tingled
in pain. My ugly body, gnarled and stiff,
ruthlessly tormented me.
I wished to jump into my father's well,
into the maw of mortality.
Instead, I dreamt of the magic stillness
of midday, when my illusion of faith
appeared before me dancing like dryads.

XXVIII

Finally, Gobbo leaves home

The falconer had released the falcon.
My father has given me up to the world!
He stood at the door of the library,
pale and unsure, eyes wide with concern.
I flew down the marble staircase, away
toward the doorway and my waiting family.
In front of my mother, whose hand I kissed,
in front of my brother, whom I hugged hard,
in front of my sister, whose hug I drank.
A thermal of anxiousness swept me
up into the waiting carriage. At last,
uncaged; at long last, golden-winged
and light, the thin air of the horizon
before me as I traveled toward Roma.

XXIX

Gobbo, the traveler

I could not experience the wondrous
beauty of Italia. I was not moved.
I read my books, travelled in their demesne.
The chiseled mountain gorges, the highland
valleys blanketed with endless
acres and acres of pasture land –
lush, green emptiness. I never noticed
the breathtaking descent toward Umbria.
Assisi, on the hill, conjured nothing.
Perugia shining in the flat distance
evoked not even a stir.
Even the town of Spoleto I lost.
These cities cast no spell upon me.
Yet in Spoleto I suffered anew.

XXX

On his way to Roma, Gobbo remembers shame in Spoleto

At the inn, in the dining room, I sat
alone, hunched over the table writing
a letter to Father. In my duty
I never heard the after-dinner noise
of the other guests. At my corner seat
I attended to my words, nothing else.
A rowdy pride of cubs, locals, spied me,
culled from the herd, exposed, oblivious.
Young lions always look for easy prey.
One priest gleefully pawed me with insults,
frivoling with me, a hunched oddity.
Well, I am no one's sport. My snarling quip
stunned him into silence. Still, his scratching
ripped me. Shame, my old wound, opened wider.

XXXI

Gobbo on his desire and his deformity

Desire is a city and I have roamed
its streets since my youth. They've been deserted
for me, always, as I hobbled along
the cobblestone alleys of Roma,
a diseased spectator to affection.
The urbane looks of cultured ladies rip
the day and tear through me as they stride past.
When you are disgusting, a defect, hope
is useless, nothing but a splintered crutch.
And love…well, love becomes blemished,
a deformed longing, a misshapen fruit.
The ripest, the roundest of them
hang hidden beyond my reach. So, I ache,
fraught with hunger.

XXXII

Gobbo contemplates his first trip to Roma

I did not study the landscape. I read
the books I brought. An edition
of Lucian, Don Quixote, manuscripts
still unfinished. And some Greek, of course.
My mind, the window that I gazed through,
revealed familiar geography,
the philological terrain of words,
whose chasms, farm land, and hills
fashioned the Fertile Crescent of my thought.
So famished for freedom, so excited
to leave my family, my home, my town
the fearful naif ventured out, sensitive,
afraid. With words, I sheltered my travel.

XXXIII

In Roma, Gobbo's expectations are shattered

How those cobblestones bruised my soles,
how every throb shot aches
of disillusionment straight to my heart.
I felt strangled in a despair
whose coils squeezed the air out of the delight
of escaping the watchful eyes of home.
Noble Roma crushed every ambition.
The fine fabric of my admiration
met with indifferent stares from scholars.
I attended no soirees. Art's parade
passed by without me. Such discomfort itched,
and I scratched with scorn. I was not well heeled,
I did not see my own naiveté;
no social graces. I was left alone.

XXXIV

An eminent philologist searches for and finds Gobbo

I found him in a palazzo's garret.
I thought I would find a seasoned scholar.
Instead, a young man, not yet twenty-five
bent over a desk, writing carefully
in a notebook, turned and gazed at me.
This fragile, hunchbacked genius, this self-taught
lover of words and ideas, whose school
was a home library and whose teachers
were the classical books he devoured there,
sat in the gloom, shrouded in rank neglect.
A few bashful words fluttered between us.
Later, I learned that he wrote poetry.
I should have known his imagination
traipsed ancient ruins, bottomless dreams.

XXXV

Gobbo at odds with the world

Shame is standing in an empty hallway.
Shame is standing in the hallway, aghast
as words scorify your heart, acid words
of a husband who does not want you
paying a call on the lady, his wife.
I did enter, and I was most polite,
though I vowed never to enter again.
I stand outside; I observe the movements
of people inside, their busy gestures
dancing a two-step with the foreign smiles
of listeners in the warmth of food and wine.
A baleful lingering coils around me,
a thick vine that strangles thin hope.
I am nothing – without love, without love.

XXXVI

Gobbo makes love to himself

Alone in bed at night, before sleep comes
the warmth in my groin nestles like a cat.
I stroke my pet with an easy rhythm,
one hand following its purring contours.
Only then do I conjure the soft thighs,
quivering breasts rubbing against my chest,
arms holding my waist tight and, oh, fingers,
that lightly trace, oh, a trail on my cheeks,
and, oh, my tongue that licks her full lips, oh,
wet with the urge, oh, to bite my mouth, oh
how I plunge into her, thrusting, thrusting
until I lay gasping, empty and spent,
my heart slowing as I turn to cushion
my head on the pillow, my soft lover.

XXXVII

Gobbo weeps at Tasso's grave

I cried at his tomb. I chronicled it.
I relished my tears falling as I knelt
at the stone slab. A rapt moment, when
I understood the immortal truce of death
stilled those armies of anguish that battled
on the plains of his soul. Tortuous wounds
no longer bled his imagination.
Fate wrestled him, and he surrendered.
He was a poet, and I wept for his life.
Consolation is a mausoleum,
more beautiful than the unearthed ruins
in that city. Standing there, I wondered
if the truest pleasure could be this:
that poets live on in their obscure graves.

XXXVIII

Gobbo realizes he will leave Roma

Reality wavered like a mirage.
Every spectacle that I witnessed
twisted into frightening shapes.
I lost my equilibrium, so sick
with meager prospects, with crumpled visions
of city life and its slick vanity.
My wild hope for rife routine took off,
running away at a gallop.
I barely caught my breath as it bolted
back to the safety of thought, reason's barn;
I tumbled off, panting, trembling.
I know. I should have snaffled this pony.
Yes, my foolishness mirrored
my body and my world, where hope was doomed.

XXXIX

Homesick, Gobbo bids good-bye to Roma

When the last bell tolls, the carnival ends,
the crowd disperses, the mass of people
melt back into the individuals
they always were. I never could carouse
with the revelers. I never could play
a part or dance wearing a grotesque mask.
I am a mask. I play my role for life.
I was ready to leave for home,
sick for the mutterings of my small town:
the whispers of church-goers, the cobbler's
muffled tapping, the wood-knocks of a loom.
You think it strange that I yearned to capture
back home what escaped me here? Not to me,
the disenchanted one, the broken one.

Act II

XL

At home, Gobbo turns from poetry to philosophy

Disillusionment, the Devil's pitchfork,
stabbed my mind. I began to rake
through my life, to discard my illusions.
I began to write out my sadness
in that bitter house I called my home.
I hoped to capture the pain of my life,
to ensnare the ravenous wolf with words.
Truth is the world that Philosophy dreams
during its deepest sleep. I tried to dream
that sublime dream, to snatch a slivered glimpse
of that world with my imagination.
But my mind was no deft hunter, the traps
set in the underbrush of my heart
though baited with Desire, sprang on nothing.

XLI

An eminent aesthetician discusses Gobbo's philosophy

Clearly, the man is tortured, his malaise
an acrid pollutant that seeps down deep
into the well water of his spirit.
His philosophy? A beautiful bile
of words that corrodes happiness, leaves us
rimed with the rust of his own bitterness.
Thus, it might be best to view his thinking
a dungeon and his dogma chains
that locked him alone with his regret.
Life, woeful, an agony, he reasons,
exsiccates all hope from the heart of man.
His dialogues, composed of words that dive
and swoop in swift, angled turns like swallows,
chatter in their woe. His misery soars.

XLII

Gobbo: *Ex Nihilo*

My pessimism boils, a bubbling vat
of hopelessness, a cauldron filled with pain.
To feed on such a diet is to eat
nothing. That is what I do when I think –
I endure the famine that is living
with this watered-down broth called logic.
I swallow hard. I am a nervous mind.
Though thirsty for sips of life's worthiness,
all that I find when I search for such brew
are flagons of illusions, a harsh drink
that I let spill on the floor.
My sole vision: a desolate landscape
where drought-ridden reality lies scorched –
singed trees, black ground, splintered shadows. No men.

XLIII

Gobbo: vox *clamantis in deserto*

Listen, I know philosophy. I know
my view of human nature frightens you.
What the world becomes is its own problem.
I seek some Truth. No, I do not presume.
Should my thoughts make a difference to you?
I see life's pain everywhere. I see
with the eyes of a poet, with luster.
My imagination is my sole hope,
a fabulous world of miniatures,
of primeval spirits, rabbits and birds,
a chthonic dream, a child's penchant for play.
My ludicrous attempts to trap logic
in my dialogues, minor salvation.
What can a poet of suffering do?

XLIV

Gobbo reflects on his two years at home

I, the family recluse, lived in peace
even though I felt I lived in a vault,
dead to life for never having known it.
Interred at home, I withdrew to study
and to write my book. When I could not write,
I paced and paced the room. Daily, I walked
the sides of nearby hills, slopes of hay fields,
a solitary dot moving slowly,
in silent, steady motion like a star
arcing through the night. I enjoyed my thoughts
for I had nothing else. And what were they?
My reliquary of insights
where votive candles of passion burned
and icons of happiness lay buried.

XLV

Gobbo assents to surprise visitors

Opportunity, that whimsical guest,
appeared at the house one day, formally
dressed as a letter from my publisher.
Chance, his shifty comrade, traveled with him
as a request to translate Cicero.
I welcomed these two pilgrims openly
then I hastened away with them, leaving
my home for tightly governed Milano.
So this house, where I fell in love with words,
their histories, their sounds, their meanings,
where I wrote in several languages,
this house that had ensnared me for so long,
I fled, but this time with Father's blessings.
Quite soon, my pen would dance on a new desk.

XLVI

Travelling to Milano, Gobbo stops in Bologna

For ten glorious days, happiness
fed me. I was a mettlesome *vespa*
buzzing around the city hovering
over its courteous society
as though it were a well-ripened melon
whose juices I could suck all day.
I flew from friend to new friend circling
the town in dizzying embroidery.
Kindness grew beneath every arcade
and I gently alit on their flowers.
The human heart, like a bowl of fresh fruit,
lured me with the succulence of hope.
People liked me. I was no hornet,
ornery and pitiless. I could live.

XLVII

Gobbo recounts his winter stay in Bologna

I lost two expensive coins, my students
of Latin, so I was left scrimping.
I pawned my watch to buy some provisions.
If I could dine with friends, I brought my food —
pecorino, some olive oil, figs —
gifts from my father. Though the cold carved
me up, a soprano's singing chilled me
worse than the Bologna winter. Her voice,
from the infernal theater adjacent
to the house, pierced the walls of my bedroom.
But her eyes, her eyes warmed my soul. Glowing eyes.
I will never forget their smoldering.
Yes, my vagrant stomach wandered hungry,
but my spirit dreamed, sated and cozy.

XLVIII

Gobbo feels kindness and happiness

Fortune's radiant smile had gladdened me.
My sister wrote once that Angelina,
our former housemaid, lived in Bologna.
So happy to see me was she, her face
flushed pink like a sunset cloud. She asked me
to dinner, and my luck took the shape
of tagliatelle. Fresh ribbons
of macaroni softened my dour heart
so that, over time, I consented to
unconsenting acts with a buoyancy
that burnished the charm I seldom displayed.
For Angelina, I wrote a sonnet
to her young priest. For Angelina, too,
I became godfather to her son. *Bontà.**

* Goodness

XLIX

A friend comments on the personal habits of Gobbo

Everyone knew him, and everyone spoke
of his annoying habits. We endured
his incessant headaches and shrouded him
in darkness to sit alone with eyes shut.
He complained about his constipation
as much as he complained about the noise
or the sunlight or the cold wind, or heat.
The man had an incredible craving
for sugar. Spoonful upon spoonful poured
into one cup. He would mete out one pound
of it for every six cups of coffee.
The man savored the sweet syrupy taste
as much as he savored the aftertaste
of his life, that most acrid of flavors.

L

A friend comments on the unsavory personal habits of Gobbo

He could be quite disgusting. We suffered
his quirks. He was preoccupied
with private thoughts. Oblivious to tact.
He blew his nose with his scarf; he spit out
pasta on his sleeve. He let his snot cake.
When he spilled food on his shirt, he ignored
the stains. And he would silently sit
at the table, morose and impatient.
He would snap his fingers to break the mood.
What an ugly sound, those fingers crackling!
His loud snorts when inhaling a pinch of snuff
signaled his displeasure at our witlessness.
But – his smile enchanted us with a spell
that bedazzled anyone at the table.

LI

Gobbo reads a poem in public

Reading one's own words aloud? Pestilence.
Boring, boring, boring. Punishment.
The listeners, those untrained dogs, twitch
on their haunches, nip one another, yawn
and softly growl. Everyone is a poet
with a poem to read aloud to others –
a habit that chokes the curious.
Even so, my stance did not deter me.
I took my turn. I followed the dashing
drake to whom I'd dedicated my poem.
I, with threadbare cravat, without bearing,
read a poem to the audience, dully.
The piece lacked backbone, lacked melody,
stumbled, and finally fell dead on ears.

LII

Gobbo denies being in love with Contessa Teresa

I relished my time with Teresa but
I never loved her. Yet she was my life,
briefly. Her graceful gestures seduced me.
When I read my poems to her, she would sob.
When I stood conversing with her, amid
the teeming literati that swam through
her fashionable salon, a rapture
permeated me with the conviction
that her gaze could stanch my wounds.
The gift of her noble stare buoyed my soul.
I floated beyond Orion's thin belt.
She acquainted me with Serenity,
whose protective arms engulfed me,
though it was a transient embrace.

LIII

Gobbo reveals his scorn for Contessa Teresa

The truth scars stark shadows that slice
the back streets of Bologna, and truth be told
I came to scorn this frivolous woman.
I tell you: Teresa pawed my spirit.
Rumors have my heart aflame, me flinging
myself at her knees, so delirious
with ardor the servant had to bring me water.
Not true. I wanted her friendship.
Ecco tutto.* Onlookers watched with pleasure
how the flitting socialite sashayed
with the hunchback, teasing his gallantry,
only to swirl blithely away from me.
Their laughter rumbled in my head; I cringed
and ducked away from those peals of thunder.

* That's all

LIV

Gobbo returns to Palazzo Leopardi

Two beasts chased me to the safety of home.
The weather mauled my health with fierce claws,
shredding the muscles of my well-being,
so that nasty creature, Doubt, could swoop down,
feeding on my brain, its prized carrion.
So, I sought solace in my antique home
sheltered away from Nature's ruthless fiends
where I could study and sleep without fear.
But in this world, there is no shelter
from suffering. I trembled and shook
in that frigid house until my curses
fell prostrate on the floor, splintered and broke.
At twilight, cocooned in a carpet,
icicles hung on thoughts of escape.

LV

Gobbo offers sweets instead of stones

Even leaving home threatened my nerves.
Those boys, that pack of hyenas, loitered
about the town, waiting to savage me
with their taunts. They would chase me,
salivating rhymes that growled from their throats
like a nauseating chorale. They flung
snowballs with stones inside them at my head.
Once, on a moonless night, I stood facing
the pack's leader. I scuttled up to him
asking, "How can you call me such names, boy?
I am going to seek revenge on you
now. Take a look at these, some real snowballs."
I pulled out a few balls of white candy.
He snatched my offering, then fled screaming.

LVI

Gobbo ventures outside the walls of Palazzo Leopardi

The town was my sepulcher. Its people
despised my gnarled body; they shunned me,
their monster, their hermit gargoyle. Entombed
in the vitriol of my home city,
I felt as though I were shipwrecked, stranded
on some forlorn island, bereft of food.
Flee? Oh yes, this kyphotic crab scuttled
away. I survived by sidling along
the shadows cast by roof eaves. To avoid
the slithering seminarians,
I pressed hard against the walls, retracted,
with my head bowed low, motionless,
eyes fixed on the ground until they passed.
No one can contend with the hideous.

LVII

A friend tells why Gobbo never used sand to dry ink

Indefatigable. The man studied
and wrote with a frost-like intensity
that rimed every minute of every hour.
He painstakingly wrote his dialogues,
copied other works like an exiled scribe
dungeoned in a scriptorium. He worked
as though towered away in musky peace,
his fancy the furnace fueling these feats.
He copied pages! Hundreds of them! Words
surged from his pen. His dialogues flooded
the paper with a gush of ink.
While the ink dried, he'd set down his pen, grab
a nearby book, and begin learning verbs
from a new language. Sand pilfered his time.

LVIII

In April, Gobbo visits Firenze

Like tree sap, my body awoke to spring.
Like leaf buds that slowly unfold
in the fresh sun, my pent-up heart unfurled
so that I could travel again. This time
to another place my wishes hoped to lodge:
Firenze, that bouquet of a city
whose cordial fragrance of ideas, art,
and conversation wafted throughout its
zealous salons, whose writers knew my poems.
Refugees, patriots, liberals all,
infested the evenings with politics.
To be invited into this sanctum!
A journal published me. For a moment,
I glinted, a blue sky on a spring day.

LIX

A literary man offers Gobbo an assignment

"The writing of this melancholy man
did not go unnoticed by me though it bobbed
in an eddy of literature's stream
and though he abandoned the world, mostly.
He appeared at gatherings, quiet, glum,
pallid with buckled shoulders like tree burls.
I kept my eyes on this crotchety tom,
yes. I rescued him; he required kindness.
Giddy from reading his *operette*,*
I foresaw his writing for our journal,
his prose like a hermit descending
from the Apennines to rant against
our Tuscan mores, those pastures
where his rank words would gallop, unbridled."

* operettas

LX

Gobbo refuses the offer of a literary man

One must live in the world to know it.
Grotesque, an ill-made misanthrope,
a dwarf, an alien, I did not choose
to escape the world, the world forsook me.
I refused its empty kiss. I embraced
solitude, a tantalizing lover
whose whispers beckoned me to her
bewitched, craggy shores of isolation.
To write about a world I've never known?
Hermits live in the world, then they leave it.
I lack fellowship with men. Look at me.
Amid the throng, I am nothing, nothing.
Man, a bothersome gnat I'd rather swat,
a speck in this universe, disgusts me.

LXI

Gobbo ponders his seclusion even from friends

Sick, a toothache seared every thought.
Fearing dentists, I sat in my room
with pain, a loquacious visitor.
Two constant companions sharply complained –
my eyes. Their worsening predicament
soured my mood. I could walk the streets only
at night. When real friends stopped by, I pouted.
Without money or food, I retreated
into myself. My heartache imploded.
I refused all invitations, all calls.
I forfeited my pleasures: festivals,
girandole spinning, horses racing
in the streets. I wandered, isolated,
shrunken, a spiritual émigré.

LXII

Gobbo articulates his relationship with the world of man

Yes, yes, of course, I did want friends.
In my mind, surrounded by scholars,
thinkers, poets, men whose comportment danced
pirouettes with flushed conviction,
I skipped my own saltarello, hopping
in delight, giddy with camaraderie.
But the mind is a cruel Chimera
and life beguiles us. I could not conform
even if I fancied that I could. No.
I did not belong with these pretenders.
Art and Beauty were my solace, shards
of the ruined urn of human nature.
Nothing matters but these soul-throbs;
the rest is scum. I do not belong here.

LXIII

An enemy attacks Gobbo's work

My hatred for this...this warped crustacean
grew steadily in the rich soil of insult.
He deemed my notes for Cicero pompous,
likened me to a mediocre prelate.
He thought my words were unlettered peasants
trudging worked-over hills. Forgive the man?
Never. Revenge burst into my psyche
when his work appeared. I brutalized it.
I called him a frog. This amphibian,
this loathsome, lame runt, truly sickened me.
I composed a sharp ditty about him.
I tormented the odd creature in life.
I stabbed the air with the words long after
he died. One should scrape away a blemish.

LXIV

Gobbo endures his suffering and creates more

I was the Great Deformed One who lacks Faith.
I was the Great Nameless Homunculus.
I was the Great Wingless, Crumpled Cherub.
What did you call me? Mollusk? Insect? Scab?
I endured such torments. This torture burned
like seasoned logs. Its bitter heat stung
my thoughts, prickled my whole being. Its smoke,
morbid stench, drifted down into my craw.
Tell me, do you know why man lords himself
over other men? The answer is 'joy,'
the malicious dog that trots alongside
the bourgeois, growling at the likes of me.
Do you think my work, my beliefs, escaped
its jaws? *Annichilare in tutto.**

* Annihilate everything

LXV

Gobbo describes his meeting with Manzoni

Fate is a severe wind, ambushing
even those alert to its dupery.
Giordani soon provoked the novelist,
his peevish words, rustling autumn leaves, swirled
in Manzoni's face. He withstood the gust.
I retreated into a corner chair.
I watched people crowd the famous author.
I respected him; he thought ill of me.
As two ships would gam on high seas, we spoke
briefly, amid the din of the salon.
The novelist saw the curse of my spine,
nothing else. About my work, he noticed
only the words, the fine cut of their jib.
He did not care to know me, the poet.

LXVI

Gobbo, alone in his room in Firenze

Solitude, my final barricade
against the onrushing troops of malice.
There I sat, hunched over a desk, apart
from the world, stifled in the room's stale air.
The heat strangled my throat. I coughed. I sighed.
My sore eyes, small brush fires on my face,
dulled the world into griseous haze.
I forced them to read my journal scribbles.
A sinister dusk stole into my heart.
A ghost-like fatigue haunted my body.
I could not hold out there, in that room.
Life's rancorous onslaught overran me.
Defeated soldiers, tired of being tired,
will swill fetid water. I gulped it down.

LXVII

Avoiding winter, Gobbo moves to Pisa and finds peace

Winter stalked me. Worse than humanity,
it skulked close behind, spying, set to pounce
on me with icy mists and mountain winds.
Cold weather, sometimes worse than any taunt,
tortured me: my joints hardened, my lungs burned.
I spurned my home, moved to mild Pisa,
found the calm harbor of comfort:
a room, affordable with light; clothes cleaned
daily; fresh bedding; and bliss each morning –
a breakfast of cherished coffee,
darling chocolate and buttery rolls,
dinner whenever I choose to have it.
My bed warmed nightly. My boots polished, too.
A fire all-day in the grate. Sweet repose.

LXVIII

Disappointed, Gobbo's father pleads for his son's return

My dejection hung like frostbitten fruit
on a neglected orchard tree. Saddened
when he left to avoid our harsh winter,
I begged him to stay home, not to leave us
for fair weather with the literati.
I asked, 'What season am I your father?'
I prayed and prayed and wrote to him often.
I hoped that Trust and Love had ripened now
in his letters and that I might pick them
the way I picked pears out in the country.
Instead, his letters snapped like deadened twigs,
their words withered, hollowed-out husks.
I wished his heart flourished for its own sake,
for me. Oh, my son. I ached for your love.

LXIX

Gobbo, on his father's love

I love my father. I do. Love flows
through every vein, through every artery
of my warped body. My blood, infected
with gratitude for him, I would spill it
in *un attimo** so that he could feel peace.
I cannot bear the heavy cross of his love
and I will not nail myself to it. No,
I told him in a letter that he craved
more than any son could give. Still, he pleaded
tenderly for my return, downhearted.
He wishes intimacy from his son,
but childhood shapes how we love, not wishes.
What is his pain? I am. A lightning bolt
that burns a hole in his heart.

* a moment

LXX

Gobbo, on the attractiveness of Pisa

The river, my mistress, brazenly flowed
as I walked beside her inhaling
the sapid aroma of her perfume.
The mild air of this city – delightful.
It is Beauty I drank in as I strolled
through the piazzas. The crowds, the strange tongues
I heard while gazing up at palatial
windows, or into the noisy cafés,
shrouded me in the haze of romantic
ardor in the middle of winter.
I did not want to leave. Sunlight
dazzling porticos, gleaming storefronts
in late afternoon, the architecture
so delicate. This life's concinnity!

LXXI

While in Pisa, Gobbo muses on the British poets

Such oddities, those British poets.
I never met them, Just as well.
Can you picture me with Byron? Can you
imagine my reactions to his dress,
his pistol shooting, his quarreling
with his servants? What foolishness!
And Shelley! One cannot speak to angels
so eccentric, so uninhibited.
He heard melodies in the tops of pines.
They must have been soft chants, vespers, I think.
And Leigh Hunt? Trelawney? Renegades.
I am not of their ilk. Genius dresses
in formal attire; propriety greets
his imagination with a handshake.

LXXII

While in Pisa, Gobbo dreams with his eyes open

Always it is the light that seduces
my senses, whether I amble along
a sunny lane or glimpse a distant field.
Always its glow evokes my far-off home.
But I walk to dream the coming spring,
to dream the distant world, the horizon
which lies west beyond the immense orchard
outside my window, the landlord's in-law,
a bright-eyed girl, young and sweet. I adored
her. The brown waves of her hair curled over
her face. Her soul spilled into her blue eyes.
Her beautiful face: I laughed to see it.
It was as though my spirit had been cleansed
with that pure, soothing lotion – innocence.

LXXIII

Gobbo writes a poem, after years

Alive again. That face of youth sprouted
buds of awareness within me. I felt
as though little shoots of vigor pushed up
out of the mulch of stupor heavy on
my breast. Stirrings – the urge to be awake.
Outside, the panorama that is life
bloomed as huge arboreal bombs of spring
exploded along the streets of Pisa.
So, I sat down to write a poem – once more.
In one April week, my senses conspired
with spring. Their delectable murmurs piqued
my fancy; my pen became its songbird.
The sweet affliction had returned to me.
Feelings trumped intellect. Resurrection.

LXXIV

Now in Firenze, Gobbo sits in a darkened room

Where I am makes no difference, does it?
Nor does the summer heat; nor does my life.
In the room, memory converged with time.
My mind erupted, spewing all the love
I ever felt high into the thick air
of reminiscence. Like molten lava,
long ago feelings flowed randomly down
the craggy mountain of the past that loomed,
unmoved in my psyche. A soft lyric
arose, and I found simple words to write.
Fields, a thrush, a handful of violets:
the ashes of recollection sprinkle
on us – Asperges of expression.
What creates a poem, can you tell me?

LXXV

Gobbo, on his brother's death and the Holy Sacrament

Pious Luigi dead. The sorrow seeped
into every organ of my body.
My brother's loss weakened me, infecting
my tears. I became a walking corpse, ill,
in pain; emptiness scalded my nerves.
Whether I observed the sacrament, or
whether I lied to father...Our motives
unfold like rituals, and rituals
flourish deep within impious sons,
who reject their honeyed transience.
My grief stoked a hatred of Florence.
I complained, complained. I withdrew,
drowning in self-pity, asked for death.
Morbidity embraced me. I stopped writing.

LXXVI

**Gobbo meets a man who could have been a real friend and
they discuss poetry**

I met a priest. He cut across my path
as abruptly as an autumn leaf caught
suddenly by a breeze sailed past my face.
We connected; his mind, independent
and lofty, spiraled in a cloud of sparks
around mine. The spirit of his sage words
exalted me above my endless pain.
We spoke of poetry and of the world,
splendid and ordered, that poets sense.
Poets fan the flames of their emotions
to a heat so intense that the iron
of each intimation can be fashioned
into words. Poets forge intuitions.
How we talked. I never saw him again.

LXXVII

Gobbo recalls his last days in Recanati

At home, faced with the onset of winter.
I draped the thought of escape like a cape
over my shoulders. It did not hang well.
My routine: long walks alone, head bowed,
hands clasped behind my waist. I followed paths
that hid me from the wind and from people.
Soon, I never left my room. I paced it
over and over. I took my meals there;
one per day, since I snacked on ennui.
Ill health, my doleful servant, tended me.
My eyeballs ached, my work plans withered,
strewn, half-plowed under the barren fields
of misery, an empty acreage
devoid of even a sparrow's lament.

LXXVIII

Gobbo cut off from his books, from his work

My mind? Parched, starved. My ideas?
Scabbed over. I could not see, could not write
a single idea, a single word.
I failed to flush either from those thickets
of despondency that had overgrown
my mind. Gone: The *Story of a Soul,*
a novel about myself, an account
of civility. Gone: the outline
for the book, *The Encyclopedia*
of Useless Knowledge. Abandoned scribbles
of a book about the passions of man,
all left in piles. Gone, too, the irony
of sitting at my desk to cherish
writing, *The Art of Being Unhappy.*

LXXIX

Gobbo's idleness yields poems

I could not rebuff the urge to write poems.
I know that from ground left fallow
the most robust grains can grow. But still,
can dejection fertilize? Can anguish?
Can a castaway, feeling stranded
in a room, instead of an island, months
and months, infuse one with inspiration?
Though I languished there, I composed four poems.
Memories burgeoned. Childhood images,
though the remotest of stars, shined on me:
the crisp air of an October evening,
the blue sky beyond the hills, out of reach,
voices mingling with the soft autumn wind.
My writing – trying to talk to the moon.

LXXX

Gobbo leaves home for the last time

Chances to leave? Yes, but no. Really, no.
Winter dragged. The cold that skulked around
the windows and the doors in my room locked
me inside, in silence, alone, with pride.
I refused a university post. Why?
Did I know about natural history?
No. Friends in Florence offered me stipends
to live while I found work. I refused. No,
still fed at home, I was not a starveling –
yet. I knew I must leave. I vowed to go,
never to return to this house, my only home.
Then, suddenly *un colpo di fortuna**:
an anonymous donor in Florence.
God threw a spear of light into my void.

* a stroke of luck

Act III

LXXXI

From behind a curtain, Gobbo's father watches his son leave, never to see him again

I do not believe that you'll understand.
I do not understand myself. My heart
bubbled with deep love, a boiling cauldron.
On the evening before he left, stricken
by his going, I walked quietly past
his room to catch a last look at my son.
I glanced at him, but he did not notice
me. I kept walking down the corridor.
In the morning, I stayed upstairs, watching
from behind the drapery as he kissed
his mother and his sister, hugging them.
Paralyzed, I could not move from my spot.
I did not take leave of my sullen son.
I spoke not one word; I never touched him.

LXXXII

Gobbo contemplates being '*Gobbo*'

I live in a world of physiques, of flesh,
a world where one's figure reflects the man.
Stature and gestures express the measured
assurance of grace, strength, and endurance.
Society demands *i gentiluomi**
to preen and pose with such an artful ease
that good fortune shines from their regal stance.
I was not built with confidence and style.
Fate mixed weakened mortar to construct me.
To all eyes, I am odious. Scoffed at,
taunted, even my friends call me '*Gobbo*.'
My hunched back and bulging chest – they rubbed
for luck at cards. I am a rabbit's foot,
a buffoon. No one believes me a man.

* gentlemen

LXXXIII

Gobbo flirts with evil

Scattered among my papers, scraps, some notes
for an ode to evil, the canniest
culprit, whom I renamed Arimane.
She prodded my mulish railings, she whipped
my hopes mercilessly. She taunted me
with desire, with pleasure, with thoughts of love.
Human beings are fools that reach for what?
Regrets? Illusions? Ludicrous ideals?
She defiles all things that men hold sacred.
I, a disciple of her treachery,
beseeched the trollop with scurrilous words,
fragments that entreated her to bestow
on me the most profound evil – death.
I cannot bear my own life; I cannot.

LXXXIV

Gobbo remarks on the last love of his life

I loved her; she remained oblivious.
She sat and teased her children as they played
at her feet, indifferent to my sighs.
The scent from the bouquets of fresh flowers
grabbed her attention more than my presence.
I sat silently, studying her face.
She never heard my passionate music –
the fiery symphony of my heart.
I love, and I am not loved in return.
Love without love returned, if it prevails,
prevails through art – my art. One quiet poem
I wrote acquitted me from loving her,
released a smile in me at her specter.
She was a phantom; phantoms do not love.

LXXXV

Gobbo recalls clouds and longings

As a child, I ran after the shadows
of clouds as they slid over the foothills,
chasing their floating roll over hedges.
They seemed blankets blackening the ground.
I pretended I might catch one. My foot,
a cat's paw, would snag its grassy fur.
I wonder if, even then, the urge
to grasp at shadows was a rehearsal
for my futile pursuit of love. My hope
for love has always been naïve, I know.
My longings, blowy as cumulus,
billowed high into the afternoon sky.
Their shapes terrified me. Their edges, ablaze,
blistered my heart. Notions lit by the void.

LXXXVI

Gobbo, on his friend Ranieri

Who was he? A Neapolitan, exiled.
Was he a hypocrite? Excitable.
Did he admire me? Yes, absolutely.
Did he see me cry? Once, behind a lamp.
Was he kind to me? Yes. Did I trust him?
Yes. Did he tend to my declining health?
Yes. Did I make his life miserable?
Yes. Did he make my life miserable?
At times. Did I feel more myself with him?
Definitely. Did I love him deeply?
Yes. Was I his lover? Certainly not.
Did he comfort my abject loneliness?
Yes, until the day I died. That is all.
True friendship fails exegesis.

LXXXVII

Gobbo in Napoli

I, a northerner, landed in the south,
in this uncouth and treacherous city.
I often thought that I would leave this place,
yet I never left. Dreams of departing
melted into the narrow, crowded streets
along with the waifs. Anxious, destitute,
my concoctions to make money with words
cooked into bitter servings of dead-ends.
I drank the vile juices of deceit once
when a publisher here refused to pay
me for two volumes of my work. Both banned,
yes, and a fine excuse to withhold funds.
In a frenzy, I waved a broom around
the apartment, ready to crack a skull.

LXXXVIII

Gobbo the neurasthenic

Worn. Emotionally ragged. My nerves
frayed and tattered as my socks. Suffering
from insomnia and dyspepsia.
Difficulty breathing. Constipated. Inflamed
eyes, mind-numbing headaches, swollen legs –
nervous breathing, spitting up blood.
My temperament foundered, sank
in the muck of irritability.
I watched my body wear itself out.
I slept the entire day; awake all night,
I dined at midnight. I dictated poems
to Ranieri. Deep into the night he read
to me. Deep into the night I buried
the misery that was my waking life.

LXXXIX

Gobbo, alone, experiences the streets of Napoli

Ah, the lively gestures of Napoli.
How the saturnalia in its streets
reeks of eels, watermelon, horse droppings.
The endless, sordid revelry of shouts
and screams. Shoving and squirming a path
past prelates and prostitutes, past monks
and mongers, past dizzying displays
of crisp pastry, past vats of spaghetti.
One day, I felt strong enough to allow
my body to be pushed in this current.
Amid the throng that carried me I spied
a friend. Twice I tried to move toward him.
Twice I failed to get close. I mouthed a greeting
as I floated away. He vanished.

XC

Gobbo, in the writer's café

Drums thumping, wine flowing, bagpipes braying –
humanity. Songs, winks and leers, I watched
it all, the unnoticed and unknown.
I viewed life once removed from life itself.
I would sit in the back of small cafés
against the wall or in a corner seat.
In the writer's café, I did not speak.
I stared down at my *caffè con zucchero**,
hunched over, sipping the black gruel.
My head, tucked low to my knobby shoulders,
made me a toad, and the writers
flouted me with the word 'toad' as they laughed.
Heavy-lidded and sore-eyed, I sat still –
eternal émigré.

* coffee with sugar

XCI

Gobbo, on some of his weak poems

Few poets in this city liked my work.
Most pronounced my philosophy empty.
They found my satires of them tedious.
My friends, too, found these pieces insipid.
Irony, a mule that refused to budge,
sat on its haunches and refused to work
in the fields of my verse. Perhaps a few
poems from a new edition of *I Canti*
took the harness well. My writing
lost luster as my body lost vigor.
My passion for life withered. Beauty dies
without passion. The marrow in my bones
seemed to mummify into ashen dunes.
My spirit sagged – a sail in the doldrums.

XCII

**A Gobbo scholar recalls one day as a young student when
Gobbo himself visited the classroom**

He was a god to us, his young readers.
Our teacher scrutinized our translations
as we sat on eggshells, watching the door.
Then it happened. He entered the classroom.
Each pair of eyes in that room fixed on him.
The Count. Poet! He, a Titan to us,
to our own inspiration. He appeared
the personification of malice.
He loomed in front of us, warped, a ghost.
No one moved, awestruck by this puny man
whose gaunt face stared blankly across the room
until suddenly an angelic smile
animated his gaze. I breathed again.
His every word enchanted.

XCIII

The same Gobbo scholar recalls his excitement at reading the new edition of Gobbo's poems

Blessed. I listened, fascinated, as he,
sotto voce, negated the ideas
of my teacher. Yes, I smiled the smile
that schoolmasters never see. We students
revered his work. My classmates visited
him. Too bashful, too nervous, too in love
with his poetry, I could never meet
the man. I carried his book of poems
everywhere. I spouted his new verse
in the streets better than the Dante rime
I had learned for class. His words made me cry.
When I read him, I explored the unknown
expanses of my heart. I sailed in
the uncharted waters of my being.

XCIV

Gobbo oscillates between the fear of death and the yearning for it

I felt it. The weight of its torment
threatened my day like the nightmare flows
from Vesuvius threatened
those who farmed its slopes. This molten menace,
so frightful to me, kept me looking back
over my shoulder, uneasy, afraid,
just as these tenants often sneaked looks back
at the peak, fearing sudden fracture.
Death: the final cataclysmic rupture.
But then: those placid afternoons when I
sat on the porch above the city, peered
over the vineyards, the rows of fruit trees,
beyond to the azure bay – celestial.
Released, my fear of death.

XCV

Gobbo, exhausted and sad

An admirer wrote a letter, praising
my poems with the poignancy of youth.
He so loved them, even in translation.
A boy enthralled with words, afraid
his feelings for my poems unworthy.
Oh, that I could write for such fond hearts.
I answered him. My deliberate hand
scribbled the truth my aching body held.
I told him that I was not a poet.
I told him that I had accomplished little.
My attempts at poems, merely this:
unfathomable prolegomena
to a life that never was, to hopeless
accolades that hovered beyond my reach.

XCVI

Gobbo, when his nights were cloudless

The stars – I wished they were the words I wrote.
The night shadows – sly, fickle illusions.
The moonlight – heaven's pallid waterfall.
My life faded into the dark vineyards,
faded into the deeper dark after
the moon dropped below the horizon
and with it any joy that I have felt
for men, for life, for my time in this world.
Then sorrow, that crepuscular insect,
fluttered around my heart before it stung
my last desire – to know no other pain
than the pain of being truly loved. Alone,
I sat outside the house. And I wondered:
can a living person know his own soul?

XCVII

Ranieri, on Gobbo's last day

At first, I did not believe he had died.
He could not breathe. His asthma awoke.
He said, 'It is time to call the doctor.'
I was afraid for him though he made jokes.
The doctor said, 'You must call a priest, now.'
My sister lifted his head, wiped the sweat
from his brow. Then his face darkened.
He stared up at me, his wide eyes frozen
open. He no longer breathed. His last words,
'I can't see you any more,' still rippled
through my chest even as his chest stilled,
even as the barefoot monk prayed for him.
I yelled my friend's name. He remained silent.
In death, he became like all men – nothing.

XCVIII

Gobbo, on his corpse

My corpse saved from rotting. My corpse detained
on route to its burial. My corpse entombed
in the church sacristy. My corpse enshrined
under a carved stone. My corpse safely buried.
My corpse become famous, its crypt opened.
My corpse found to have rotted, its bones mixed
with the crumbled wood. The skull of my corpse
disintegrated into the sordes.
The remains of my corpse's bones moved
at last to a cliff near Roman ruins.
The same stone marked my corpse. I rested there
where I once gazed over land and sea.
Legend says that Virgil's corpse lies nearby.
Poets, even as corpses, linger on.

XCIX

Nunc Dimittis: Gobbo contemplates his bones

My bones cannot pain me as they did
when I lived. What is left of them is dust,
and dust is time, those heartsick memories –
the wish to love, the wish to die, the wish
to master my unhappiness, my fate.
My fate – that my bones fade beyond time,
that I, a man destined to be woeful,
die like all creatures in this thankless world.
The pain at loving is the heart of hope.
It stopped beating for me before my bones
failed. The substance of the love I felt –
rotted bones mingled with rotted wood.
All is nothingness; that is Death's bald fact.
Still, stars glimmer. I no longer hurt.

C

In the room where Gobbo was born, his mother speaks

He had been dead for years. Then the pilgrims
arrived, those sorry fools, to lionize him
and his work. Ahi! He wasted his talents.
Do you suppose God thought him virtuous?
God watches us. He watched my son ignore
Him. To know this freezes my aching heart.
A stranger walked in, stared at a painting
of my son and told me that I was blessed
to have mothered him. I stiffened and froze.
I did not move my head. Only my eyes
raised up toward the ceiling to Him who knows
the words I whisper in prayer each day,
the words I'll whisper until my death,
the words I whisper now— 'Forgive my son.'

ABOUT THE AUTHOR

David Cappella, Professor Emeritus of English and the 2017/2018 Poet-in-Residence at Central Connecticut State University, has co-authored two widely used poetry textbooks, *Teaching the Art of Poetry: The Moves* and *A Surge of Language: Teaching Poetry Day to Day*. He won the Bright Hill Press Poetry Chapbook Competition in 2006. His poems and essays have appeared in various literary journals and anthologies in the US and Europe. His novel, *Kindling*, has been called "a powerful and devastating coming-of-age story." Visit his university web site: http://webcapp.ccsu.edu/?fsdMember=249

CPSIA information can be obtained
at www.ICGtesting.com
Printed in the USA
BVHW081430120722
641927BV00008B/331